The
Calvary Road
Study Guide

by
Rev. Stephen C. McCary

Companion to
The Calvary Road
by Roy Hession

CLC

PUBLICATIONS

Fort Washington, PA 19034

The Calvary Road Study Guide

CLC Publications

U.S.A.
P.O. Box 1449, Fort Washington, PA 19034

GREAT BRITAIN
51 The Dean, Alresford, Hants. SO24 9BJ

ISBN 13: 978-0-87508-784-9

© 1999 Rev. Stephen C. McCary

This printing 2013

Note to User

Roy Hession's book *The Calvary Road* is currently published in two sizes: trade paper ($5^1/_4$ x 8) and mass market ($4^1/_4$ x 7). As a result, though the wording is the same in both editions, the page numbering usually differs. So that this study guide may be used by anyone who has either size book, we have placed the mass market page numbers in parentheses immediately after the page number of the trade paper-size book. Example: "Reread pages 20–21 (22–23)."

•　　　•　　　•

In addition, the reader deserves a word of explanation concerning the several places where, following a Greek word, a parenthetical number is given. That is the lexical number of the word as found in the Greek dictionary which is appended to *Strong's Exhaustive Concordance of the Bible*, where its fuller meaning and usage may be studied.

Contents

<table>
<tr><td>

**The
Calvary Road
Study Guide**

</td><td>

Introduction and Preface

This study of Roy Hession's *The Calvary Road* is a chapter-by-chapter open discussion. However, your greatest gain from this study will most likely come from your thorough preparation prior to class. Preparation should include reading each chapter assignment twice—once to observe in overview, and then again as you work through each subpoint.

</td></tr>
</table>

Working through each subpoint may include the following:
- Highlight or mark any section to which you can especially relate.
- Highlight or mark sections with which you disagree or do not understand.
- Write in the margin Scripture references that are applicable to the subpoint.
- Make prayerful introspection relative to whatever the Holy Spirit brings to the surface in your Christian walk.

1. In light of the above considerations, read Norman Grubb's introduction on pages 7–9.

2. Summarize Grubb's description of "walking in the light" on page 8.

_____

_____

3. Now read the preface, beginning on page 11.

4. Read Ezekiel 37. In the preface Mr. Hession writes that revival is a "valley full of dry bones being able to live again and stand up an exceeding great army" (37:10). Throughout the prophecies of Ezekiel, but especially in chapters 34–37, God repeatedly says, "Then they will know that I am the Lord." What does this say about the overall purpose for revival in an individual's life?

_____

_____

5. On pages 16–17 (18–19) the author comments about the "necessary attitude of heart" for the reader of *The Calvary Road*. Meditate on this section and ask, "What is it about *me* with which I am dissatisfied?" Consider the relationships around you—your mate, your children, your parents, your friends, your supervisor, your employees; consider your walk with the Lord. (No one should feel obligated to discuss this openly during class.)

Brokenness

<table>
<tr>
<td>

1

The
Calvary Road
Study Guide

</td>
</tr>
</table>

Chapter 1 will prove to be foundational for the entire study. Having read through the chapter twice (once to overview and once to carve and digest), consider the following:

1. Last week our key area of focus dealt with revival. Based on pages 19 and 20 (21 and 22) as well as the book's Introduction, write your own definition of personal revival.

   _____

   _____

   _____

2. On page 19 (21) Mr. Hession describes revival as the state of being in a "right relationship" with Christ. On that same page he states there is a prerequisite for entering into this right relationship. What is that prerequisite?

   _____

   _____

3. Please fill in the blanks. The author describes this will (of our proud self) as "the hard _____ self, which _____ itself, wants its own _____, stands up for its _____, and seeks its own _____."

4. Time for an honesty check! It is easy to see these "flaws" of self in others, but what about you? Stop and consider your own self-centered will, as seen by God and by those close to you. How are the following manifestations of self-centeredness seen in your life?

   A. Unyielding:

   _____

   _____

   B. Self-justifying:

   _____

   _____

   C. Wants its own way:

   _____

   _____

D. Stands up for its rights:

_____

_____

E. Seeks its own glory:

_____

_____

5. Reread pages 20–22 (22–24).
   A. Write the author's definition of brokenness:

   _____

   _____

   B. Consider seriously the "worm" analogy. Be prepared to discuss this next week in small group. (Reading Psalm 22 may be beneficial.)

6. On pages 22 and 23 (24 and 25) the author addresses "dying to self."
   A. Read the entire fourth chapter of Second Corinthians.
   B. Now reread pages 22 and 23 (24 and 25) of *The Calvary Road*.
   C. Is there any conflict between the author's "dying to self" and 2 Corinthians 4? _____

      i. Are there ever exceptions to "a constant yielding to those around us"?_____

      ii. On what basis might an exception be considered? _____

      _____

      _____

      iii. If you believe there is an exception to the author's definition of "dying to self," can you prove that from Scripture? What would the attitude of that exception be? _____

      _____

      _____

7. As this homework assignment comes to a close, read Colossians 1:13–18. Afterward, pray as the Lord leads you, thanking Him for who He is and for His immeasurable grace.

Cups Running Over

Thus far in our *Calvary Road* study we have identified and defined two key factors in experiencing the reality of the Christian life. First, we have learned that *revival* is personal and daily, not corporate and seasonal. That's not to say that a community of believers cannot experience revival's effects, but revival is personal because God is a personal God. He deals with men and women "heart by heart." Second, we realize that *brokenness*—my daily response of humility to the conviction of God— is the prerequisite to personal revival. As you begin this week's lesson, read John 14:15–27 and 16:5–15; then spend a moment thanking our wonderful Lord for His presence in you.

1. Are you filled with the Holy Spirit? By simply asking that question do your thoughts tend to gravitate toward the charismatic doctrine? What do you think the author is trying to teach with the "cups running over" analogy on

   _____

   _____

   _____

2. Read Ephesians 5:18. If you have a Greek lexicon, look up the word *pleroo*, (G4137), which is translated "filled." Consider the context of chapter 5, but also look at the following verses where *pleroo* is found: Col. 2:10; John 12:3; Luke 2:40; Matt. 13:48. (Hint: For what purpose is a glass filled? For what purpose is the sail of a boat filled with the wind? Answer: For its intended purpose!) What do you think it means to be "filled by the Spirit"?

   _____

   _____

   _____

3. In the subsection "Under the Blood," the author describes sin as the following: self-energy, self-complacency, self-pity in trials, self-seeking in business or Christian work, sensitiveness, touchiness, resentment, reserve, worry. Read the footnote at the bottom of the same page. Why are these *not* merely human weaknesses, common to all, with which we will struggle throughout this life?

   _____

   _____

4. The author gives another definition of revival. "This is revival—the constant peace of God ruling in our hearts because we are full to overflowing ourselves, and sharing it [the peace of God] with others." Oh, to daily experience the peace of God! Isn't that everyone's desire? Look up the following verses and jot down your observations about the peace of God.

    Romans 5:1–2 _____

    Galatians 5:22 _____

    Ephesians 2:13–14 _____

    Philippians 4:7–9 _____

    Colossians 1:20 _____

    Colossians 3:12–17 _____

5. Colossians 3:15 says, "Let the peace of God rule in your hearts." The Greek word for rule is *brabeuo* (G*1018*) which means "to arbitrate" or "to govern." In light of Roy Hession's statement on page 28 (31), "Everything that disturbs the peace of God in our hearts is sin," and also considering his example of the indwelling Holy Referee (Spirit), what does this mean in your life? With family members? At work? Within the body of Christ?

    _____

    _____

    _____

    _____

    _____

    _____

    Wouldn't it be great if, when sin was crouching, the Holy Spirit would blow an audible whistle for everyone to hear? I believe we would all develop hearing problems from the constant shrill, don't you? Thankfully, God speaks to our hearts personally. Every day this week, ask Him for an increased ability to hear His whistle blow. It may be a glaring violation, or a series of self-centered thoughts or behaviors. Either way, "Let the peace of God rule in your heart."

The Way of Fellowship

Revival . . . Brokenness . . . Filled with the Spirit. Three terms which now have new meaning in this Calvary Road experience.

Revival: the practical and potentially daily reality of being made usable again (by His power) for the eternal purposes of God.

Brokenness: the daily, moment-by-moment response of hu-mility to the conviction of the indwelling Holy Spirit (my will broken to His will).

Filled with the spirit (as wind fills a boat's sail): being continually guided by the Holy Spirit toward God's ultimate purpose.

1. Reread the first paragraph on page 31 (35) and reflect on the closest relationships of your life. You know—those where conflict tends to arise! Conflict can be so complicated, but it is rooted in the basic truth stated on this page. From where does conflict come? What is at its root?

   _____

   _____

   _____

   _____

2. Study 1 John 1:1–9. Verses 3–4 indicate that our hope for fellowship with one another is based upon the fellowship we have with the Father and His Son. In verses 5–7, what do the following words mean? (Be sure to remember the context.)

   Fellowship _____

   Walk _____

   Walk in the light _____

   Walk in darkness _____

   Cleanses _____

3. Spurgeon defines walking in the light as "the willingness to know and be known." Hession adds that we "are not going to hide our inner selves from those with whom we ought to be in fellowship; we are not going to window-dress and put on appearances; nor are we going to whitewash and excuse ourselves. . . . It means, too, that we are not going to cherish any wrong feeling in our

hearts about another, but we are first going to claim deliverance from it from God and put it right with the one concerned."

A. What are the vulnerabilities you may face in walking in the light with those close to you? _____

B. Is there a difference between "just being honest" and "walking in the light"? _____

C. Read 1 Corinthians 13. Is walking in the light different than the instruction to love? _____

4. In the subsection "No Bondage," Hession writes: "Then when God guides us to open our hearts with others . . ."— page 37 (42). This seems to indicate there is a place for the proper timing of much open communication. Why would proper or improper timing be worth considering? Be sure to test your answer for scriptural integrity. _____

_____

_____

_____

5. What does the author mean by "drop the mask"? _____

_____

_____

_____

As you pray this week and consider all you are learning, ask the Lord to especially open your heart for understanding what it means to walk in the light.

The Highway of Holiness

<table>
<tr><td>

4

The
Calvary Road
Study Guide

</td><td>

As the author states, chapter 4 is written in picture form in order to further express the simple truths of the victorious Christian life. How did that opening paragraph on page 39 (45) strike you? *Is* "utter simplicity" at the core of the gospel? If you haven't read the entire chapter, be sure to do so before going further. Have a pleasant trip down the "Highway of Holiness"—and let's hope we can all "stay for a while."

</td></tr>
</table>

1. In your own words, express the simplicity of living the victorious Christian life. What are the biblical truths which make it "simple"? _____

   _____

   _____

   _____

   _____

2. In your own words, express the simplicity of *not* living the victorious Christian life? With an honest heart, ask yourself: Why do the simple truths seem powerless for me at times? What is at the core of my foot slipping off "the highway" at any given moment? _____

   _____

   _____

3. Reread the subsection entitled "A Low Door." Having previously discussed this in chapter 1, explain the phrase, "To be broken means to have no rights before God and man"—page 41 (48). Be sure to review the author's definition of brokenness. _____

   _____

   _____

   _____

4. Read the last paragraph in the subsection "The Gift of His Fullness." What is required to experience this "plain day-to-day living of the life the Lord intended us to live"?

   _____

   _____

5. In the subsection entitled "Off the Highway," Mr. Hession pictures Satan
    beside the road, shouting at us, but not being able to touch us. Reread this
    section. Remembering the definition of brokenness (my will being broken
    to the conviction of the Holy Spirit), how will "staying broken" keep me
    on the highway? _____

    _____

    _____

    _____

6. You know, it is somewhat easy for us to recognize and admit God's right to
    convict and correct us by His Spirit. However, I find it difficult at times to
    accept God's intended correction for me, delivered through the heart and
    words of a friend, a spouse, a colleague or an acquaintance. Since sin makes
    me hide—resulting in pretentious, mask-wearing ways—I too am off-balance
    in my relationships with others. How should my "broken" attitude respond
    when confronted with truth from another? _____

    _____

    _____

    _____

The Dove and the Lamb

1. In a brief sentence, express the heart of the author's illustration of the Dove and the Lamb. _____

   _____

   _____

   _____

   _____

2. Under the subsection "The Humility of God," Mr. Hession states that the main lesson of this incident is that the Holy Spirit as the Dove could only come upon and remain upon the Lord Jesus because He was the Lamb. He lists three qualities of the Lamb's disposition. Why are each of these qualities important to the Holy Spirit's working in a person's life?

   A. Humility _____

   _____

   _____

   B. Submissiveness _____

   _____

   _____

   C. Self-surrender _____

   _____

   _____

3. In this same section you were directed to read Galatians 5:22–26, contrasting the fruit of the Spirit of God with the works of the flesh (5:19–21). According to the context, why is it necessary to allow the Holy Spirit to produce His fruit in you? Jot down your answer according to the following verses.

   A. verse 24 _____

   _____

   B. verse 25 _____

   _____

   C. verse 26 _____

   _____

4. Concerning the following descriptions of the Lamb of God, be ready to discuss their general application, but allow the Lord to speak personally to your heart regarding each of these.

A. The Simple Lamb _____

_____

_____

_____

B. The Shorn Lamb _____

_____

_____

_____

C. The Silent Lamb _____

_____

_____

_____

D. The Spotless Lamb _____

_____

_____

_____

E. The Substitute Lamb _____

_____

_____

_____

In the final subsection of this chapter, the author calls each of us to be ruled by the Dove (Holy Spirit). What a contrast! We would rather be ruled by the mighty Lion of Judah—by the King of Kings. Or maybe by some external list of *dos* and *don'ts*. Or maybe by "my accountability group"! But not by a Dove! Remember, the goal of the Christ-life is *not* to be a better Christian. It is to be conformed to the image of God's Son by the Holy Spirit's conquest of self. Victory is not me overcoming my sin; victory is Jesus Christ overcoming me. When He overcomes me, moment by moment, the only biblical response is humility and brokenness, which brings on the much needed grace of God. GLORY!

Revival in the Home

"Satan is attacking America . . . one family at a time." I recall that line from a Bill Gaither musical entitled "Bind Us Together," written and recorded over thirty years ago. If revival is to mean anything to the body of Christ, it must first mean something in the home. It is in the home where relationships are experienced in blatant reality. Sadly, however, family relationships are not always experienced according to honesty or biblical truth. Have you ever spent time in a foreign country? Each country has its own unique culture—that is, the way life is "done" or lived in that country. As we begin this week's study I'd like to challenge you to consider your home life (either that of your present family or the one in which you were raised) as a culture. What were some of the "laws" that no one challenged? What were some of the "rules of the road" that everyone knew they must follow? How was conflict dealt with? Was (or is) your family an open or closed "society"?

1. Pay close attention to the first two subsections of this chapter. Be ready to discuss the simple yet profound reality that a God-centered home is the only home where true harmony can predictably exist. _____

_____

_____

_____

_____

2. The author identifies two problems which prevent the God-centered home from prevailing.

    A. "The first thing that is_____ with so many families is that they are not really _____ with one another." Read thoroughly the section entitled "What Is Wrong with Our Homes?" Jot down your observations and be ready to discuss this during small group time. _____

_____

_____

_____

_____

_____

B.   "The second thing that is wrong with our homes is our_____
to really _____ one another." Do you really believe the opposite of
love is hate? Do you asccept the premise that not loving, according to First
Corinthians 13, is hating? Summarize your thoughts and be ready to discuss
them in class. _____

_____

_____

_____

> *Roy Hession has identified two profoundly intricate yet simple
> realities that prohibit true oneness. I am speaking of oneness
> with the Lord, oneness with my family and oneness within any
> relationship in my life. Both deal with my self-absorption —as
> seen in my unwillingness to predictably walk in truth (honesty,
> openness) and my unwillingness to predictably love God, my
> mate/family and others.*

3.   So if we know the problem, what prevents us from walking in oneness? What
prevents us from experiencing revival in our homes? Prayerfully and carefully
reread the subsection "The Only Way Out." List below the points identified
and be ready to discuss them in small group. _____

_____

_____

_____

Ask the Lord to instruct you as to how to experience revival in your home. By His
grace and according to His truth, trust Him.

The Mote and the Beam

7

The
Calvary Road
Study Guide

It is so much easier to see the faults of another than to see my own. Likewise, it is easier to excuse my own mistakes (shortcomings, sins, etc.) than to overlook the "inexcusable" ways of another. Pride and prejudicial thinking are the twin "bad boys" of this week's study. Prior to reading chapter 7 in *The Calvary Road*, prayerfully read Matthew 5–7. Ask the Lord for a gracious measure of His wisdom.

1. Mr. Hession points out that the removing of the mote (speck) from the eye of your neighbor is a valid and needed ministry of service. Look up those passages he mentions and jot down any thoughts that may enhance your understanding of this week's lesson. Other "one another" passages may be helpful also.

   Romans 15:14 _____

   Hebrews 10:24–25 _____

   John 13:14 _____

2. So, what is the beam (log)? Explain the author's view of the beam. Is the beam always as obvious as the metaphor might suggest? _____

   _____

   _____

   _____

3. Reread the section "Take It to Calvary." Look at this through the reconciliatory eyes of our loving God. Describe the entire process of "taking it to Calvary" which Mr. Hession discusses in this section. Be ready for discussion.

   _____

   _____

   _____

Remember, this is accomplished only by the work of the Holy Spirit. Contrary to all the "yeah, but" examples which run to my mind, the Holy Spirit reminds me that God's economy is different from mine. "Be ye holy; for I am holy" (1 Pet. 1:16, KJV).

Are You Willing to Be a Servant?

<table>
<tr><td>**8**
The
Calvary Road
Study Guide</td><td></td></tr>
</table>

In Bill Hull's book *Jesus Christ, Disciplemaker*, speaking of Jesus' final, pre-death encounter with the disciples, he writes: "The Master wanted to show his men what kind of character a leader must have in order to effectively influence others. Jesus now began to cram three years into three hours." And He began this all-important encounter by washing their feet. What a picture of servanthood! What an *unglamorous* life Jesus portrayed the life of a Christian to be. Sometime this week read John 13–17.

1. As chapter 8 opens, the author identifies three preliminary understandings for our look at biblical servanthood. In the space below, jot these down and be prepared to discuss them.

   A. _____

   _____

   B. _____

   _____

   C. _____

   _____

2. Mr. Hession goes on to identify five marks of the bondservant. As we ponder each of these, allow the Holy Spirit to have His way with deep conviction regarding the way each of us seems to consistently hold on to our rights, especially within relationships at home and work. Don't forget that humility is first an *attitude* before it is an *action*.

   A.   First of all, the bondservant must be _____ to have one thing on top of another _____ upon him, without any _____ being given him.

   NOTES FOR DISCUSSION: _____

   _____

   _____

   B.   Secondly, in doing this he _____ be _____ not to be _____ for it.

   NOTES FOR DISCUSSION: _____

_____

_____

C. Having done all this, he must not _____ the other with

_____ .

NOTES FOR DISCUSSION: _____

_____

_____

D. Having done all that, there is _____ _____ for pride or

self-congratulation, but we _____ _____ that we are

_____ servants, that is, that we are of _____

_____ _____ to God or man in ourselves.

NOTES FOR DISCUSSION: _____

_____

_____

E. The _____ that doing and _____ what we

have in the way of meekness and _____ , we have not done

_____ stitch more than it was our _____ to do.

NOTES FOR DISCUSSION: _____

_____

_____

3. Reread the section describing the Way of the Cross.
    A. Why is the Way of the Cross the way for each of us? _____

_____

_____

    B. Identify the unwelcome intruder: _____

_____

    C. Explain the role of repentance and why we shall not enter into more
    abundant life merely by resolving that we shall be humbler in the future.

_____

_____

_____

_____

_____

We are bondservants of the One who delivered us from the domain of darkness and transferred us to the kingdom of His beloved Son. (See Col. 1:13–18.)

The Power of the Blood of the Lamb

"What can wash away my sin? Nothing but the blood of Jesus. What can make me whole again? Nothing but the blood of Jesus." We sing it and say "Amen." We preach it and say "Amen." To truly understand the power of Jesus' blood is to understand that I am powerless apart from it. Powerless to save myself, for sure, but also powerless to walk daily (and humbly) in the light; therefore, my ongoing fellowship with God is possible only by the power of the blood of the Lamb.

1. In their context, study the following passages and make observations regarding the blood of the Lamb of God.

    A. Colossians 1:20

    _____

    _____

    B. Colossians 1:14

    _____

    _____

    C. John 6:54

    _____

    _____

    D. Revelation 12:11

    _____

    _____

    E. 1 John 1:7

    _____

    _____

    F. Hebrews 9:14

    _____

    _____

    G. Hebrews 10:19

    _____

    _____

2. "So we see not merely is He the Lamb because He died on the cross, but He died upon the cross because He is the Lamb" (page 79) (96). From the sub-section entitled "Whence Its Power?" explain this phrase.

    _____

    _____

    _____

    _____

3. Carefully read Philippians 2:1–9. Based on Christ's humility, God the Father highly exalted Him and "bestowed on Him the name that is above every name." In verse 3, Paul commands believers to "consider others more important than [themselves]" by exhibiting from the heart the same attitude the Lord Jesus Christ did when He considered us so important that He went to the cross.

    A. Does this passage teach that true humility will *guarantee* us God's blessing? _____

    B. If you believe it does guarantee God's blessing, might that blessing be fully realized only when a believer reaches heaven? _____

    C. Are you content to humble yourself because God commands it, expecting no earthly blessing in return? _____

    D. Will those who know you best consistently see the fruit of your contented heart? _____

4. Of course, the prerequisite for Christ's exaltation was death to His human will (see Luke 22:42). Reread the subsection entitled "Are We Willing?" and summarize what it takes to walk with His peace in our hearts.

Is walking with God and enjoying His peace enough exaltation for you? Doesn't our flesh "require" a bit more exaltation than merely the peace of God ruling our hearts? I know I struggle with this at times. Oh, it's not that we think we should be exalted super highly, but there's something about our flesh that desires recognition by others—usually those higher up on the spiritual, social or economic ladder. I share this not to make you feel guilty, but that we may bow down to the One who gave His life for us and confess that our sins are simply the result of our self-centeredness.

Protesting Our Innocence?

I recently heard Chuck Swindoll state that a problem with most Christians is that we are too familiar with the Bible! Sounds strange, doesn't it? However, he was attempting to communicate that all too often we read over familiar passages without allowing the Holy Spirit to teach us *something new today*. That's the way I feel about this chapter. I am so familiar with what the Word of God says about "the flesh" that sometimes I fail to recognize it as *my* flesh. It is so much easier to condemn the flesh of the tax-gatherer even while, in my condemnation of another, *I* stand guilty before God!

1. In the subsection "God's Picture of the Human Heart" it is apparent that my heart (the rational, free-will part of man), in its unregenerate or flesh-controlled state, is opposed to God. In the space below, jot down your observations of the Scripture listed and be prepared for discussion.

    Mark 7:21–22 _____

    Galatians 5:19–21 _____

    Jeremiah 17:9 _____

    Ephesians 4:22 _____

2. In the same section, the author writes: "The simple truth is that the only beautiful thing about the Christian is Jesus Christ. God wants us to recognize that fact as true in our experience, so that in true brokenness and self-despair we shall allow Jesus Christ to be our righteousness and holiness and all in all—and that is victory." According to what you have learned in this study and from what you already know of the Word of God, what are "true brokenness and self-despair"? Define them and give a practical example how each would be seen in your life.

    True Brokenness: _____

    _____

    _____

    _____

    Self-Despair: _____

    _____

_____

_____

3. Reread the section "Making God a Liar!" Summarize the lesson in this sec-
    tion. _____

    _____

    _____

    _____

4. Haven't we all said, when speaking of someone prominent in our eyes who
    has sinned, "It's just not like him to do something like that!" What are we
    really saying? Consider *that* as you summarize the lesson in the subsection
    "Justifying God."

    _____

    _____

    _____

    _____

5. In the section "Peace and Cleansing," the author states that we have a choice
    "to protest our innocence and go down to our house unblessed, dry of soul,
    and out of touch with God. Or to justify God and to enter into peace, fel-
    lowship, and victory through the blood of Jesus." Reread this section and jot
    down the apparent prerequisites to entering into peace, fellowship and victory.

    _____

    _____

    _____

    _____

    _____

Thank you, Lord, that in spite of me You loved me enough to give Your very life, the
only righteous life ever lived, in order that I may have everlasting peace with You.

Forty Years Later

As our last week of this study comes to a close, can you identify with the title of this book *The Calvary Road*? The road to Calvary wasn't a pleasant road for Jesus, but it was a necessary road. Necessary not in *our* plans, but necessary for God's ultimate purpose. It is never pleasant to walk the road that deals with my pride and prejudicial behavior, but it is always a necessary walk because God's ultimate purpose is that I be conformed to the image of His Son. That means I must decrease and that He (Jesus) must increase. And to do so I must choose to recognize that I (the *old* I) am crucified with Christ: nevertheless I (the *renewed* I) live; yet not I, but Christ liveth in me: and the life which I now live in the flesh I live by the faith of the Son of God, who loved me, and gave himself for me (Gal. 2:20, KJV).

FIRST INTERVIEW

Roy Hession quotes Charles Finney as saying, "Revival always presupposes a declension. Therefore if a man can't own up to declension, he is no candidate for revival personally"—page 92 (112–113). Be prepared to discuss the heart-beat of this quote. Read Romans 7.

_____

_____

_____

_____

_____

SECOND INTERVIEW

Be prepared to discuss the continuous effects of revival. This interview is some-what of a review of chapter 2, "Cups Running Over."

_____

_____

_____

_____

_____

_____

Third Interview

In this interview the question is asked, "Do you sense Christ's blood being operative in your life on, say, a daily basis?" What would it mean in *your* life to sense Christ's blood being operative on a daily basis? Be prepared to discuss the essence of this third interview. Sometime this week, read Romans 5.

_____

_____

_____

_____

_____

_____

_____

There are unsuspected forms of self. We think we know most of them, don't we? Are we willing to allow those closest to us to lovingly correct us? In order for the Calvary Road to be operative in our lives, it takes Jesus Christ to be the Lord of our lives moment by moment.

> But if we walk in the light as He Himself is in the light, we have fellowship with one another, and the blood of Jesus His Son cleanses us from all sin.
> (1 John 1:7, NASB)

This book was produced by CLC Publications. We hope it has been life-changing and has given you a fresh experience of God through the work of the Holy Spirit. CLC Publications is an outreach of CLC Ministries International, a global literature mission with work in over fifty countries. If you would like to know more about us or are interested in opportunities to serve with a faith mission, we invite you to contact us at:

CLC Ministries International
PO Box 1449
Fort Washington, PA 19034

Phone: 215-542-1242
E-mail: orders@clcpublications.com
Website: www.clcpublications.com

DO YOU LOVE GOOD CHRISTIAN BOOKS?
Do you have a heart for worldwide missions?

You can receive a FREE subscription to
CLC's newsletter on global literature missions
Order by e-mail at:

clcworld@clcusa.org
Or fill in the coupon below and mail to:

**PO Box 1449
Fort Washington, PA 19034**

FREE *CLC WORLD* SUBSCRIPTION!

Name: _____

Address:_____

_____

Phone: _____ E-mail:_____

GO DEEPER WITH

WE WOULD SEE JESUS
the follow-up to *The Calvary Road*

George Verwer says:
"I would recommend every believer to read *The Calvary Road* and follow it up by reading *We Would See Jesus*."

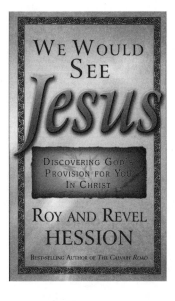

We Would See Jesus
mass market
ISBN 978-0-87508-586-9

We Would See Jesus Study Guide
by Linda Traughber
ISBN 0-87508-475-3

Available at your nearest bookstore or from CLC Publications:
Phone: (215) 542-1242
E-mail: orders@clcpublications.com
Websites: www.clcpublications.com